In the Midst of the Storm

In the Midst of the Storm

COVID-19

Monique M. Milner

Wethersfield, CT
www.DizaJoy.com
change@dizajoy.com

In the Midst of the Storm

First Edition

Paperback ISBN: 979-8-9851093-5-1
eBook ISBN: 979-8-9851093-4-4

All glory, praise and honor belong to our Lord and Savior, Jesus Christ.

To our Mom
Our Warrior
Our Everything

The one who showed us the true meaning of strength, endurance, and courage. The great magnitude of love, life, family, struggle, joy, tears, sunshine, and rain. You are always in our hearts.
Thank you.

"We love you, always"

Prologue

The content is graphic and heartbreaking, but it needs to be told. To protect privacy, identities, and identifying details, the names and some dates have been changed. We need justice! We need change! This hospital health care system must change to ensure the safety and well-being of every patient who comes into this facility. I can speak only about our experience at this hospital during the COVID-19 pandemic. No one should ever have to endure the horrific experiences that my mom and our family endured. My mom, 66 years old and full of life, was first admitted into the hospital on March 12, 2021.

Fast forward to April 22, 2021; during her hospital stay, my mom developed another horrible cough and a lot of phlegm in her chest, which caused difficulty breathing. On a good day, she could sit up and try to cough and clear the phlegm that had built up in her chest. At times, she even used the mouth suction the hospital provided to clear her throat. On a bad day, depending on the medicine she was given, she required a lot of help, patience, and monitoring. She choked and gagged on the phlegm.

This particular morning, I went into my mom's room as usual; her nurse was leaving the room as I entered. I said good morning to my mom, letting her know that I was there. I joked with her every day, asking her: "Can I get a few moments to get myself together?" Patience was not one of mom's virtues. I made every effort to keep our routine the same every day. I put on her gospel music, cleaned and disinfected her room, talked to her, washed her face to remove all of that stuff from around her mouth, wondering why no one else saw and removed it before me, moisturized her lips, and combed her hair, at least let her keep her dignity. Nights were tough for mom because no family members were there to help her or see what was going on.

I noticed that morning that she had restraining mittens on her hands. I was upset, but I always tried to stay calm around my mom. Remember, I said earlier that her nurse was leaving as I came in. If my mom was so calm, why was she wearing restraining mittens? She was just lying there, not doing anything. I told my mom: "Let me get those off you." I took the restraining mittens off her hands, which were weak and limp. I was saddened, but I had learned my lesson the hard way. I could file a complaint, but all that would have accomplished was retaliation against my mom. Instead, I continued to make mental notes about what was going on, and I journaled throughout her stay. I continued praying that she would be transferred to the hospital we requested soon, as she needed to get out of this toxic environment.

My back was turned to my mom as I was cleaning the counter near her bed. I heard her coughing. I told her: "It's okay, cough it up, get it out of you." I always coached her through it. But I soon realized that this cough was different; it was a choking, gasping sound, with a struggle. I turned to look at my mom, and I noticed that she had tried to sit up, but only her head was raised. Something was wrong. I moved closer. It took me a minute to process what I was seeing. Her cheekbone was more defined. She was gasping. Then, it clicked.

"Oh my God," I screamed, "I got it." I had to dig my fingers between the oxygen tubing and my mom's cheekbone and neck just to give her some space to breathe. Her oxygen tubing was setup like a noose. The tubing usually goes in the nose, divides, and goes behind the ears and down the side of the neck. There is a little piece that tightens the tube by sliding it up or down in the front to keep the tubing in place. My mom's oxygen tubing was in her nose and went behind her ears. Follow me on this. The tubing from her left ear went all the way down, under, and around her neck like a rope to her right side. The tightening piece was pushed tightly into her neck on her right side, then both pieces of tubing went completely under her pillow, then out the top end of her pillow, and off the back of the bed. The main cord, the one that went from left to right and that was acting as a rope, was stuck on something behind my mom's bed. My mom's body weight was resting on the pillow. Her oxygen tubing was being used as a noose. I know that the tubing was stuck or secured tightly on something behind the bed because, even though I am pretty strong, when I pulled on the tubing, there was no slack.

Let's do a recap.

When my mother was coughing, she tried to sit up, but she could not because she was tied down by her oxygen tubing. She could only get her head up and forward. Mom was fragile. She could not hold the weight of her head up, so her head dropped, which activated the tubing like a noose. The tubing dug deep into her neck, causing her head to be suspended in midair and was cutting off her airway. Shame on them! Someone placed that tubing around my mom's neck, without a doubt. Was this why she was wearing restraining mittens? So many bizarre incidents like these occurred at this hospital that made me wonder if this was what really happened.

How many more people did this hospital annihilate or try to eliminate in the middle of the COVID-19 pandemic and then say it was due to COVID-19? I saw, witnessed, and documented the wrongdoings committed to my mother in this hospital. The horrific experiences that my mom endured were only routine for this hospital.

Getting back to the noose, I desperately looked for the call bell, but it was nowhere in sight. The call bell buttons on the bed were not working. I was on the right side of the bed, holding the tubing that was around my mom's neck. I saw the call-bell cord coming from the wall on the left side of her bed. I tried to follow the cord from the wall using only my eyes. I still could not see the physical call bell, but I knew it was on the side opposite from where I was standing. I quickly explained to my mom: "Your call bell is on the other side." I let her know that I had to let go of the tubing for a second to run to the other side to push the call bell and that I would be right back. It broke my heart, but I had to call for help.

I found the call bell on the floor. In case of an emergency like this, my mom could never have reached the call bell on the floor. I pushed it and immediately put my hand back between the tubing to relieve some of the pressure on her neck. I let my mom know I was taking pictures. This was wrong and totally unacceptable. The nurse came in, and I went off. "Why is my mother hanging by her oxygen tubing? It's around her neck, under her pillow, running down the back of the bed, and caught on something." The nurse helped me get it loose, but, as I stated before, she was leaving my mom's room when I came in. She had evaluated my mom before I got there. How did she not see that the tubing was not placed correctly? It took me a few minutes to figure it out, but she is the nurse. Nursing is her job; she should have caught on when she did not see the tightening piece and cord in front of my mom's neck. Or was she the one who put the tubing in the position where I had found it? Months later, while on the phone with my sister, we were still replaying everything that took place. I am going through pictures on my phone; the first date I saw the restraining mittens behind my mom's chair was 04/20/2021. That same day I realized there were foot restraints hanging from my mom's bed. I had to bring the call with my sister to an end. I cried after I hung up. I had an epiphany they were restraining our mom's hands and feet. Shame on them! That is how they were able to tie her oxygen tubing around her neck like a noose and put it behind her pillow. My mom would have never held still and allowed them willingly to hang her.

I asked the nurse: "Page the provider, nursing supervisor, everyone. This is unacceptable." When the nurse coordinator came, I told her what had taken place and let her know that this was unacceptable. My mom could have died if I had not arrived when I did. She apologized, stating that they take pride in patient safety and that she would make sure that this did not happen again. I told her that it takes only one incident of negligence for someone to die. The medical provider and team of students came in; they were doing their normal rounds. I was still boiling mad, so I asked him if he knew what had just happened.

He said, "Yes," and that he would get to that in a moment.

Chapter 1

My mom went to the hospital on March 12, 2021, in respiratory distress. The urgency of her distress left the ambulance no choice but to take her to the closest hospital. Ever since I was a child, I knew that only people who were dying went to this hospital where my mom was admitted. And that was only because they could not make it to the next hospital. This hospital's reputation was that bad. It is also a teaching and training hospital; there is nothing wrong with that. But we did not want mom to be used as an experiment. My mom would never have chosen to be treated at this hospital.

The hospital said that she had pneumonia, and they did a COVID-19 test. Two days later, my mom's test came back positive for COVID-19, which was devastating to the family. I was on a telehealth visit with my doctor when my sister called me twice back-to-back because I couldn't pick up. On the third call, I told my doctor: "One moment, something must be wrong." That's when my sister told me that mom had tested positive for

COVID-19. My sister was upset and crying; she was in her car and had pulled over on the side of the road. I told her I would call her right back.

I am now the oldest since our brother was killed. Our family is small, and I try to keep the family together. When I got off the phone, I broke down crying and hyperventilating. My doctor on the telehealth visit was trying to calm me and help me to breathe. It was my worst nightmare come true. Mom had just moved into a house. She lived on her own; she was independent. But my mom had many health issues: diabetes, high blood pressure, chronic obstructive pulmonary disease (COPD), liver disease, and sleep apnea. We had learned recently that she also had a small aneurysm on her brain, congestive heart failure, pulmonary fibrosis, and something going on with her kidneys and lungs. COVID-19 was nothing I wished on anyone, and I knew it could be bad for my mom.

The provider let me know that my mom was able to make her own health decisions, but she chose not to, letting them know to speak to me. I was the one responsible for making all her health decisions. The providers, nurses, and everyone else involved in my mom's treatment always called me with updates, plans, questions, and so on. I always connected my sister on the line, as we are a team. The providers were trying to stabilize my mom to determine her treatment options. The provider told us that, due to her health conditions, she did not qualify for any of the normal therapy they would try on COVID-19 patients. Because of the issues with her kidneys, lungs, and liver, the therapy drugs could affect and damage those organs even more. The provider did tell us that there was a clinical trial with plasma. The provider did not know anything about it, but she would get me in contact with the provider doing the trial to see if we would like to try it.

The clinical trial provider called us back and went over what the trial entailed. I was a little familiar with the plasma clinical trial, or so I thought, due to what I had seen on TV or online. In this plasma clinical trial that they were offering my mom, there was a 50 percent chance she could get plasma and a 50 percent chance she could get sugar water colored to look exactly like plasma. The trial was to see if the patients who received the sugar water got any better, even though they knew that the sugar water does not do anything to help or treat COVID-19.

A fifty-fifty chance! What a choice. The provider also explained that no one—patients, providers, caregivers—would know which patients had received the plasma and which had received sugar water so that everything and everyone would remain unbiased. We told the provider that we would have to discuss it between ourselves and then with our mom, and we would get back to her. She setup a time to call us back.

This was sad. They told us that the only thing mom qualified for was a clinical trial of an experimental therapy with no guarantees. But they were also telling us that they could not even guarantee she would get the experimental therapy that might help. This was too much. We spoke to our mom and explained everything to her about the fifty-fifty chance. Mom said no. If there had been a guarantee that she would receive the plasma, she would have done it, but it seemed like a waste of time not to help her in her current situation since this would just provide knowledge for the future.

We were all on the same page. The provider called back, and we declined the clinical trial. Our hearts were heavy. The decisions we were making involved my mom's life. *Were we making the right decision? How could we turn down the only option that she had?* I was nervous, but I never let it show. I prayed, hoped, needed to believe, and trusted that the Lord would work it out. Shortly after that, my mom's regular provider called back. She had just gotten word from the clinical trial provider that we had declined the trial. The provider wanted to know why we had turned it down. We went over the main point. There was no guarantee that mom would get the real plasma that could potentially help. Instead, she could get sugar water, and no one would ever know. If she got sugar water, precious time would be lost.

The provider thanked us for sharing that information with her. She said that she knew nothing about the newly offered trial, as the hospital did not tell her. She also informed us that knowing the trial details; she would have decided against it also. That lifted our burden a little, knowing that we had made the same decision the provider would have if she had been in our shoes. My mom's provider then told us that she had seen my mom and that the hospital also had the initial plasma treatment with the real plasma. But mom had told the provider that she was done with plasma. We wondered why it was not offered to her before the new experimental treatment.

Chapter 2

The provider had been consulting with other providers in different specialties about my mom. They had been watching her blood levels for two days, and her levels seemed to be stable. Mom is now qualified for the respiratory therapy drugs used on COVID-19 patients. Remdesivir was an antiviral, and Toce Tocilizumab was used in combination with a high dose of a steroid, Dexamethasone. *Thank you, Lord!* They would closely monitor her blood levels and make changes accordingly, trying not to cause further damage to her organs.

Mom had developed a bad, deep cough and a lot of phlegm. We spoke to her about the therapy, and it was a go. We were excited, grateful, and we were ready. She was ready. We had a treatment plan, and we had developed a schedule.

I had started journaling for the first time when my mom was admitted to the hospital. The nurses worked twelve-hour shifts from 7 a.m. to 7 p.m. and vice versa from 7 p.m. to 7 a.m. I would speak to the night nurse every morning around 4 a.m. before they started their end-of-shift rounds, checking to see how my mom's night went, going over her blood work, and getting the plan for the day. This call also let me know who the incoming nurse and providers were, which allowed me to have the nurse page the provider when I had a question or concerns about my mom's bloodwork, especially the need to repeat an order. I was keeping track of all her lab orders and the results through her health portal app. I kept a close eye on her D-dimer, which was her blood-clotting factor, throughout her whole stay. I was worried about blood clots due to her lack of movement. I always made sure that they used the leg-compression boots and repositioned her to help prevent blood clots.

My mom listened to her gospel music regularly. She came to the hospital with her cell phone and no charger, but no worries. The nurses made sure her phone was charged every night. They had extra chargers that made it possible for the family—my sister, uncle, which is my mother's brother, and me—to video call during the day.

On March 15, 2021, They started giving my mom heparin injections in her stomach to prevent blood clots. Physical therapy and occupational therapy came in to see her. I remember them saying they would continue doing therapy with her body. At that time, her lungs were not ready, meaning her breathing and the oxygen she requires, but when her lungs were ready, they needed her body to stay conditioned so that her body would also be ready. They had gone over the potential discharge plan, which could be an acute inpatient rehab, but only if my mom could do three hours of physical therapy a day. If not, she would go to an inpatient skilled nursing rehab facility. But we were nowhere near that point; it was just information that they passed on.

During a video call with my mom, I noticed that, as she talked, she was short of breath. I informed the family to give her a break; call to check on her, but don't let her do a lot of talking. Let her save her breath. This was a big mistake because, after about two days, I noticed that some confusion had set in, and she was not able to have a complete conversation. She was repeating herself. I informed the medical staff, and they had noticed it too. On March 26, 2021, during the morning update with the overnight nurse, he let me know that, when he went into my mom's room, she was standing beside her bed, her oxygen was off, and she had voided on herself like she was trying to go to the bathroom.

In her right state of mind, my mom knew she could not go to the bathroom by herself. The nurse had her on a short oxygen cord. She had to call the nurse for help if there was a need for the bedside toilet. She would never take off her oxygen in her right state of mind. She knew the oxygen was used to help her. Even at home, she was on two liters of oxygen. The nurse informed me that the lack of oxygen might have caused the confusion. In the blink of an eye, my mom did not know her name, was not talking, was not following commands, and was unable to feed herself or eat. The provider called it "hospital delirium," which occurs when a patient is in the hospital for a long period of time. At that time, she had been in the hospital for less than a month. The nurses make their rounds about every two hours, as she was on a COVID floor. They popped in sooner when we were on a video call, and I saw my mom was having difficulty. I had to hang up in order to call the nurse for assistance. This happened when she had difficulty breathing, or she was choking on the phlegm, which happened a lot. I spoke to my sister and my uncle. I asked the nurse if they had a baby monitor or anything we could use or buy and bring in as a monitoring device. There was not, so we decided to use her phone. The nurse brought the charger into her room and kept her phone connected to the charger. We kept the video call open like a monitor.

I let the nurses know that every time they went into my mom's room, they should call us day or night to open the video again if the phone was off. We now had a monitoring system, and we could watch and talk to her if needed around the clock. Our continuous use of the phone made a tremendous difference. My mom went from blinking to following commands, from one word to a conversation. She knew her name, she fed herself, and she was starving. *Thank you, Jesus!!* The family said this could not happen again. We had to keep her engaged in conversation throughout the day. When I talked to the provider, she was amazed. She informed me that my mom's turnaround was because of us being there on camera, talking to her, and engaging her. The hospital tries to keep the patients out of delirium, but they do not have the staff or time required to be with the patients continuously.

I was so proud of us, and that came from the provider. That did not stop the thoughts in my head about all those lives lost to COVID-19. I was saddened. Is this what it was like? The chaplain stopped by. We were trying to get my mom's affairs in order legally, with her advanced directives for health care. The chaplain had stopped in earlier, but my mom was a little altered at that time. This time, it was a go. She was alert, and my sister and I were on a video call. The chaplain went over the forms; my mom answered all of the questions, and she signed the documents in the presence of witnesses. They put a copy in her chart, and my mom permitted them to mail my sister and me a copy.

The first part of my mom's stay at the hospital was touch and go. We hit some bumps in the road, but they seemed to work themselves out. The providers were listening to the family's input because we knew her best. I remember my sister and I talking about her stay at the hospital and our concerns from the past. I said that it seemed like they were doing reasonably well at that point. Maybe a leopard can change its spots after all. We were grateful that everything appeared to be going okay and that she was still alive. The therapy treatments were coming to an end, and she was coming off the steroids. Life was good.

Chapter 3

Case management started talking with us about the discharge plan. At this time, my mom was still on a short oxygen cord and required assistance from the nurse to get out of bed to use the bedside toilet. The option that we were rooting for was an acute inpatient rehab facility. My mom had to be able to do three hours of physical therapy a day to qualify. I spoke to my mom; she was strong and determined. She said that she could do it, and I knew she could. An inpatient skilled nursing rehab facility was not an option because my mom did not want to go to a nursing home.

I asked for the names of the possible rehabilitation facilities, so we could do some research and read up on them to make an informed decision. There were not many, I think, only three that took recovering COVID-19 patients. We made our choice. We were waiting for the insurance authorization. But we were one step closer to getting my mom back home, where she and we wanted and needed her to be. Home. However, a day or two later, my mom called me. She was distraught. She said that a lady had just left her room after telling her that the insurance company had denied her transfer. She needed to get up and get moving so that they could send her to a low-grade facility. Sometimes, it is not what you say but how you say it. I told my mom to calm down, I would take care of it, and I would call her back.

Immediately, I called the case manager, whom I will call Case Manager A. She was the only one I had spoken with about a discharge plan. I asked Case Manager A if she had just left my mother's room. Case Manager A said no. I told her that I was upset because everyone knew that they were to communicate with me about my mom's care. How dare someone upset my mom, knowing that her oxygen dropped and that she had problems breathing when she was upset? I told her what was said and informed her it was totally unacceptable. I asked her who just left her room.

Case Manager A went into my mom's chart and said that it was a Physician Assistant (PA) and gave me the person's name. I will call this person Physician Assistant Provider 1, mind you I had been waiting for Case Manager A to return my call about the approval status. I had to hear it from my mom after Physician Assistant Provider 1 upset her so badly. Then, hesitating, Case Manager A told me during our phone conversation: "Yeah, the insurance company denied the authorization." I asked, "Why?" She was still hesitating like she had to gather her thoughts. Then, she said that the insurance company denied it because my mom did not need that level of care. I said: "Let me understand this. The provider sent over the paperwork letting the insurance company know what was needed, but the insurance company overrode the provider and decided that my mom does not need that level of care? Is that correct?" She said, "Yes."

I had never heard of an insurance company telling the provider that is treating a patient what level of care the patient needs. Case Manager A then informed me that I could appeal the decision, and I did. Case Manager A informed me they would do a peer-to-peer appeal, which I found out later meant that the hospital provider would speak to the insurance provider on behalf of my mom and the appeal. I asked for the insurance company's number, so I could call them.

I then called the insurance company. I was transferred to my mom's insurance navigator. I explained what happened and asked how the insurance company can override the provider. Her insurance navigator checked the authorization notes and informed me that the insurance company denied the claim because the documents received did not support the need. She added that the peer-to-peer appeal, which was the hospital's provider's appeal to the insurance company's provider, stated that my mom did not need the level of care that required that she be seen by a provider daily. These were the reasons given to me for the claim being denied.

One of the qualifications for acute inpatient rehab was the need for the patient to see a provider daily, which required supporting documents. I explained to the navigator that, to that day, my mom had seen a provider daily because her labs were always off from evening to night to morning. A provider was constantly coming to see her, adjusting and changing her medications. I filed my first complaint with the insurance company against the hospital. I had no time for their lies, games, and foolishness.

Then I called Case Manager A back. I said: "You told me the insurance company denied my mom's claim because they said my mom did not need that level of care. But the insurance navigator went through the authorization notes. The hospital did not send over documents to support my mom's need to see a provider daily. Also, the peer-to-peer provider did not even support my mom's need to be seen daily. Before I knew that the authorization was denied, physical therapy (PT) evaluated my mom and took acute inpatient rehab off the discharge plan. We were only offered inpatient skilled nursing rehab due to my mom's oxygen and mobility issues." Finally, I asked for a new physical therapy consult.

Case Manager A informed me that they usually do not do another physical therapy consult after a patient is in discharge status. I asked: "How do you get an accurate treatment plan on a patient from a few days ago? Since then, my mom has gotten stronger." Case Manager A did not answer my question, but she did setup another physical therapy consult. The nurse had even informed me they put my mom on a long oxygen cord, and she was able to walk to the bathroom with assistance. They had done another evaluation, and it seemed to be good. She was able to walk across the room. Physical therapy said she was strong, although her oxygen did drop; they bumped her up a little from four to five liters of oxygen. She recovered, then they turned the oxygen level down. It was looking promising; physical therapy knew to call me after therapy to give me an update.

During this time, I spoke to the provider, questioning the denial based on the paperwork and provider that did not support my mom's need to be seen by a provider daily. While on the phone with the provider, something else occurred with her lab results; I think her platelets were very low. The provider said that they would make sure to resubmit the paperwork to reflect that my mom did need to be seen by a provider daily. Case Manager A was aware that the provider was resubmitting the paperwork to reflect the need for a provider daily. It seemed like we were on the same page again.

The next time my mom had physical therapy, she complained that they were doing too much. While she was trying to do therapy, the nurse was trying to do a finger stick. My mom said that it seemed like they wanted her to "Get this, do this." They did not give her time or a chance to catch her breath. My mom said that physical therapy (PT) should be calling me. I will call this person Physical Therapy A. My mom stated that she did well and that Physical Therapy A had said that it seemed like she could do three hours of therapy.

Physical Therapy A called. Having done physical therapy with my mom, her recommendation was still the same: inpatient skilled nursing rehab. I asked: "How is that possible? I just got off the phone with my mom, and she told me that you said she did good." I was talking to Physical Therapy A on my earpiece. "Can you explain to me why from the beginning, when my mom was at her worst, her options were acute inpatient rehab or inpatient skill nursing rehab? But now she is only being offered the nursing rehab?"

Right when I asked the question, someone else asked me a question. I put Physical Therapy A on mute while I answered the question I needed to answer. Then I heard Physical Therapy A whispering to someone over the phone, saying: "She wants to know why in the beginning her mom was offered … and now …". I was trying to listen. Then I heard her say: "I am just going to tell her I got a page, and I will call her back."

What do they tell you about an open mic? I unmuted my phone, and my voice was shaking. I said: "I am back." She said: "I got a page." I said: "No, you did not. What is your name? I heard what you said, and I will be filing a complaint." Physical Therapy A did not say a word. I was so mad that I disconnected the call.

To make a long story short, shortly after our conversation, I called and spoke to patient relations. I voiced my complaints from Physician Assistant Provider 1 on down to the open mic and how I felt that the hospital was conspiring and colluding against my mom for reasons unknown. I now had three open complaints—nursing, case management, and physical therapy. Patient relations assured me that someone from each of the three departments would get in touch with me.

My mom's request for the same acute inpatient rehab facility was denied again by the insurance company. The hospital sent the paperwork over correctly with the need to see a provider daily, but the hospital put my mom's oxygen requirements higher than what they really were, which caused her not to qualify for that facility. According to the hospital's paperwork, the oxygen levels that my mom required were higher than the facility's oxygen capacity. I spoke with the provider about her increased oxygen levels. Her listed requirement of six liters was new to me, and the provider did not know of it either. The provider stated that if my mom had required six liters of oxygen, Physical Therapy A should have reached out to the provider because the provider may have needed to make some adjustments.

I also spoke to my mom about her oxygen levels because she was alert and oriented; she could see her oxygen levels. She informed me she was not on six liters. She was ranging three to four liters while sitting, and, while she was standing and moving around, they increased her to five liters so that she could recover faster. I also spoke to my mom's nurse about the oxygen levels, and she also was unaware. Only Physical Therapy A supposedly saw and documented the high levels. The weekend was approaching, and everything went wrong over the weekend. For some reason, on Friday, my mom was cleared for transfer, but by Monday, she was not medically cleared.

Chapter 4

On March 31, 2021, I spoke to Case Manager A's supervisor and voiced my concern about how I felt they were conspiring and colluding against my mom. I said that I did not want Case Manager A involved in my mom's care any longer. Moving forward, Case Manager A and her manager were always on the phone together while going over my mom's treatment plan.

I also spoke to Physical Therapy A's supervisor. I informed her of my concerns with them conspiring and colluding against my mom. I mentioned the phone conversation during which Physical Therapy A whispered to someone as if she was trying to get guidance and said that, at no point in time did she tell me someone else was in the room or a part of our conversation. The supervisor of Physical Therapy A agreed that she should have informed me that someone else was in the room. She also apologized that I felt like they were conspiring against my mom. Unknown to Physical Therapy A's supervisor as she continued to speak, she only confirmed my suspicion of conspiring and colluding when she told me who was in the room with Physical Therapy A during our conversation. It was Case Manager A!

Imagine this, Physical Therapy A was in the room with Case Manager A, but when Physical Therapy A's supervisor asked about the whispering that I heard during our phone conversation while the call was muted, Physical Therapy A informed her supervisor that she and Case Manager A did not say anything. I did not think about this until later. *Were they calling me a liar? How did I know someone else was in the room if they did not say anything?* At first, I had only suspected that they were conspiring and colluding against my mom, but now I knew they were. *Why would Physical Therapy A have to get guidance from Case Manager A? Were they trying to read from the same script, be on the same page?* Physical Therapy A evaluated my mom. That is her job, what she does for a living. She should have been able to answer my question without assistance. Physical Therapy A and Case Manager A have two different jobs.

I also informed the supervisor about the denial incident with my mom's paperwork and the peer-to-peer provider. The supervisor also informed me who the peer-to-peer provider was (hospital provider to insurance company provider). The peer-to-peer provider was Physician Assistant Provider 1. This was further confirmation that they were conspiring and colluding against my mom. Physician Assistant Provider 1 was the same person who went into my mom's room earlier and upset her by telling her that the insurance company had denied her transfer, as she needed to get up and get moving so that they could send her to a low-grade facility.

You have to be kidding me. The same provider did the peer-to-peer and stated that my mom did not need to be seen by a provider daily, even though she did in reality. Conspiring and colluding. I told my mom: "We have to get you out of here to move forward." To get her home, the skilled inpatient nursing facility was the only option. To weigh all of our options, we asked the provider if it was possible for my mom to be discharged to her home with twenty-four-hour home care. The provider did not feel comfortable, and my mom's condition did not permit her to be discharged home with twenty-four-hour care.

I also spoke to the supervisor at the nursing facility and voiced my concerns. I asked if my mom could do everything, including physical therapy, in her room. She would be on a recovering-COVID-19 wing at that facility. I did not want her to go out and interact with other patients because her immune system was too vulnerable. The supervisor informed me that they would be able to accommodate her. That was good news. She would also have a shower in her room. My mom was excited about that. Even though she had a shower in her room at this hospital, they would not let her shower. I asked many times about a shower, as I knew that it would make my mom feel better. She loved being clean. The initial response was that they would try to make that happen that day, but it didn't happen. Then it was her oxygen, or it was not a good time. By that point, she had been about three weeks without a shower, only bed baths.

The bottom line was that they were short-staffed. We asked the nursing facility supervisor that if my mom was not happy at the nursing home or if things were not going well, would she be able to check herself out at any time. The nursing supervisor responded that if things are not going well, they would like to talk about them. But yes, my mom would be able to check herself out. By that point, it was coming up on the weekend, and this was my mom's third discharge plan. We were waiting for the insurance approval authorization and glad to be moving on.

What happened? By Monday, my mom was not medically cleared to be transferred. Here we go again; things constantly took a turn. I asked them constantly to repeat certain labs, especially her D-dimer blood clotting factor. Even though she was on blood thinners, she was at high risk for clots. Her oxygen and lab results were all over the place that weekend. I stayed logged into the app via her health portal so that I could see all of her labs ordered, results, and so on.

We thought she was on the road to recovery, but her cough came back, and this time with a vengeance. The phlegm was horrible. During many of our video calls, we had to disconnect the call to be able to call the nurse to go in and help my mom. Again, the nurses are supposed to do their rounds every two hours. It was nerve-racking. When they left the room, we knew we had one hour and fifty-nine minutes before they returned. On many occasions, right after they left, we witnessed my mom choking and gagging on her phlegm. When she was alert, she could push the call button, but thank God we had the video call setup when she was not. The hospital was short-staffed, and they could not give my mom the attention she required. Responsibility to keep her safe fell on her family.

We took turns pulling shifts. I mean literally all three shifts, my sister, my uncle, and I. My sister had the third shift covered. When her shift of watching our mom was over, she connected my uncle or me, and vice versa. Twenty-four-hour monitoring by video call because this hospital had staffing issues. They had no kind of accommodation in place for patients who required more care. We did not mind; we had to do what was needed and had to be done. The bottom line was to keep our mom, his sister, safe.

We were not able to visit due to the hospital's COVID-19 policy. The cough was so bad that my sister and I thought she had gotten reinfected with COVID-19. She was still on a COVID floor. They did another X-ray. Then the hospital informed us that she could have pneumonia again, so they put her back on steroids and an antibiotic. I remember that her lab results had many flags, either high or low. I always looked up her results online to see what they were and what the cause was so I could discuss it with the provider. When I researched her lab results, I kept coming across hypoxia.

That night, my mom was different. She was repeating herself, not having a full conversation again. The next day, April 7, 2021, I noticed it had gotten worse. I had already informed the medical staff, and they informed me that she had stopped voiding and that they had to put a catheter in that evening.

Chapter 5

I got a call that same evening that my mom required more time and oxygen, and they were going to transfer her to the Progressive Care Unit (PCU), where she could get the care that she needed. The nurse-to-patient ratio was better. I was nervous, as they had gone over the oxygen requirements for each floor earlier, and the PCU was too close to ICU for comfort. We had to continue praying and keeping hope alive. I asked that they please call me before she was transferred, so I could explain to her what was going on. I asked that they make sure she had her phone and update the new floor about what we had been doing with her video calls, gospel music, updates, and so on.

I fell asleep, woke up in a panic, and called my mom's nursing station. She had already been transferred; they had not called. The nurse's station on my mom's former floor transferred me to her new floor. I spoke to her nurse to see how my mom was doing and let her know I had requested a call that I did not get. The nurse asked: "You wanted a call at midnight?" I let her know that my mom is my mother twenty-four hours a day.

I wanted to video-chat with my mom, but the nurse told me my mom was confused and that they had to restrain her. This was the first time in my mom's almost a month-long hospital stay that she was restrained. The nurse also informed me that there was no charger for her phone and that they were unsure how to provide gospel music for her to listen to. Suddenly, the phone disconnected. I was devastated. My mom was confused, around no person or voice that she could recognize, in a quiet room, and restrained. That broke my heart. The world has been dealing with COVID-19 for a year. We must find a way to help patients and families to stay connected and offer music therapy. We did not change hospitals; we changed floors. This was crazy. It was like day and night. I called the nursing station back. I thought that the PCU nurses would be more caring, compassionate, and have more empathy. Instead, they were burned out, rude, had no compassion, no empathy, and did not care.

Remember, my mom did not come into the hospital with her phone charger, but the other floor had a cord, and, from the beginning, they took her phone out of her room every night to charge. Then we had set it up as a video monitor. But, on this new floor, coming up on a month of my mom being in the same hospital, they informed me that, because she was a COVID patient, they could not take her phone out of her room to charge it, nor could the cord go into her room.

They did not know of a way to offer music in her room because she was a COVID patient. I said that the other floor played the music from the computer. They informed me they could not do that. I complained that her family needed to be there. She was nearly a month into her stay and was still not able to have visitors. I told the provider that I was willing to sit outside her door and help. This floor has a lower ratio of patients to nurses, but they still did rounds only every two hours. They still did not have the time or staffing that my mom required for her medical condition. They used the restraints regularly so that they would not have to deal with her.

I sent a phone charger to the hospital within the first few days after my mom was transferred to the new floor. I needed to see my mom. With the restraints, not talking or seeing anyone she knew, I knew it was wearing my mom down. We knew and saw that there were many occasions when my mom needed help during the two hours between rounds. With her choking on all the phlegm build-up, it was hard to watch and harder to hang up the video to call the nurse's station because we knew that she could not connect to us again. Again, it was the same stuff, just on a different floor.

On one occasion on this new floor, as we were on video, she was restrained and had an itchy nose. To scratch her nose, she had to sit herself up, bend down, and pull up her restrained hands to her nose. Her oxygen tube came out of her nose. I called the nurse's station, and the secretary put me on hold. When she came back on the line, I informed her that my mom's oxygen was out and asked if she could have the nurse go into my mom's room to help. We hung up the phone. I was pacing anxiously. I called back a few minutes later. I asked the secretary if she had let the nurse know my mom's oxygen was out of her nose. The secretary told me no, she was busy, she had gotten a call. I repeated that my mom's oxygen was out: "We know she needs that to breathe. You need to let the nurse know, and you should learn how to prioritize a patient with no oxygen or a phone call. Which is most important? My mom's oxygen will drop and drop quickly." The secretary must have looked at the monitor at the nursing station that was connected to my mom. She sarcastically stated her oxygen is fine. I repeated to the secretary can she let her nurse know.

I asked again about my mom having visitors, and I asked about her having a sitter and told the provider, whom I will call Provider 2, that the family was willing to pay for it. Provider 2 stated that was not possible due to COVID-19. PCU was worse than her previous floor; they kept my mom restrained, and eventually, she could not sit herself up to cough the phlegm out. She literally was choking and lying in her phlegm. I did not notice it at the time, but physical therapy and occupational therapy had stopped coming to do therapy. I talked to Provider 2 about my mom's safety because something had to change. My mom would die if they kept this up. She was past the COVID-19 phase. Provider 2 said that he would see what he could do.

He talked to me about doing another COVID test. If it comes back negative, we would have to repeat it again. Two negative tests could change my mom's status, and then the family may be able to be by her side and help. The next day on a video with my mom, her nurse told me that the provider was ordering a COVID test and asked if I knew why. I did know but chose not to answer her. Nurses on this floor had such a negative vibe. Nursing and the medical staff were aware that we were trying to get my mom COVID cleared so that she would be able to have a family member by her side to help. I was confused. He was the provider, and she was the nurse. It seemed like she was questioning him. The nursing staff was aware of the two negative COVID tests rule-out process. I wondered why my mom did not deserve a chance to have family by her side. They say nothing beats a failure but a try. Why not try? Then she said: "It seems like a waste of resources. It is just going to come back positive."

Help me, OMG, in front of my mom. I could have told her something, but not in front of my mom. *What are they pouring into her soul? Even though she is not talking, she is still breathing. She is still there. She can still hear.* Shame on her. Since mom was transferred to PCU, they had always talked as though she was not there. When I called to get an update and ask how she was doing they would say: "She is here, but not here." I am still trying to figure out what that meant.

I would always say: "Act like this is your mom in this bed. What would you do?" While on a video call, Provider 2 came in, and my sister and I talked about my mom having a right-sided facial droop. We asked about a stroke. Provider 2 assessed her and said that mom did have a delay when he asked her to release his hands. It took a little bit for her to process it, but nothing indicated that she had a stroke. They had informed me that same day that my mom would not eat. The next day, I was on a video call when her lunch arrived. I observed before I spoke to see how things played out.

The nurse opened the Ensure, tapped it on my mom's lips, and said: "Let us try to drink some Ensure." My mom did not open her mouth. The nurse put it down, picked up a spoon full of eggs, and did the same, tapping it on her lip. My mom did not open her mouth. The nurse said, "We will try later," and took the tray away.

I said: "Wait a minute. Ma, you look thirsty." Again, my mom had a lot of phlegm. I asked the nurse if she could wet a rag and wipe her mouth, and she did. I said: "Let's start with some water. Your throat must be dry. Milky Ensure is not going to help." I asked the nurse to put some water in a cup with a straw, and she did. Then I said: "Ma, try that cold water."

The nurse put the straw on my mom's lip. It took a minute, but she opened her mouth and guzzled that water. Out of her lunch tray, she drank sixteen ounces of fluid and ate some eggs.

"I think we, the family, should be on the payroll by now. I informed the nurse that, in case you did not know, Provider 2 said my mom had a delay. Have patience."

It was easier and quicker for the nurse to say that mom did not eat than it was to take the time that the nurse needed to help her eat. With this hospital being short-staffed, it did not help. Who suffers? My mom, the patient. Imagine someone bringing you food three different times a day. You are starving and ready to eat. But they do not give you a chance to eat because, for whatever reason, you cannot respond fast enough to open your mouth. They remove the food, so you did not eat by choice but by force. That is cruelty.

On another occasion, when my uncle and I were on a video call with my mom, her nurse came in to assess her and asked: "Do you know your name? Do you know where you are?" My mom didn't say anything. The nurse said: "You are in the hospital. You caught that bad disease everyone is dying from."

I was confused. That was not comforting to hear or something that would help her remember. Everyone on the PCU floor spent a lot of time telling my mom she had COVID-19.

Then the nurse said: "It is okay if you do not remember. You just woke up; you were on a machine that was helping you breathe. It will take a while for your body to process things."

I said: "What are you talking about? My mom has been awake the whole time. She has never been on a ventilator." Now I asked myself if my mom got the wrong medicine; did she get the medicine for the patient who had just come off the ventilator? Is that why things looked the way they did?

Another time, while on a video call with my mom, we noticed something was wrong. She kept looking at the door, and we kept trying to engage her in conversation. She looked at the camera with a serious demeanor and said: "Shh, they are listening." I made a mental note. We continued trying to talk to her. Something was different. She was watching their every move outside her door.

I said, "Ma, it is okay."

She looked at me and said in a stern voice: "It's not okay, you don't see what's going on in front of you."

Later that night, we noticed that mom saw things that were not there. I spoke to Provider 2 about my concerns. I started with my mom seeing things, but Provider 2 told us that this could be a side effect of the different medications she was on combined with the steroid. I also told him about the nurse questioning him and basically stating that my mom was a waste of resources. I can still hear her say that. Who says something like that in front of the patient? It still breaks my heart. Even though my mom was unable to talk, she could still hear. Provider 2 apologized.

This was the first time my mom's lab results were lit up all over like a Christmas tree. I had continuously mentioned hypoxia and worried about blood clots, but the providers were not worried about either. It seemed like they stopped testing because they didn't care to know what was going on. My sister and I were concerned about our mom's safety. We requested a transfer to another hospital. Because my mom had started seeing things, they had a psychologist evaluate her. The psychologist said that it was delirium. I stressed to them that this was different.

My sister and I were concerned because, at around the same time, she stopped talking, voiding, and eating, and now she was seeing things. Our video calls were not as consistent as when she was on a regular floor. This new psychotic medicine was just sedation. It made her zoned out like a paralyzing drug. My mom could never tolerate pain, and she had a low tolerance for medicine in general.

Chapter 6

The next day, April 11, 2021, while we were on a video with my mom, we noticed that she had developed a fear. You could see it on her face. Obviously, something had happened overnight that we could not see. First, she was continuously looking at the door with fear. Then it was whenever the nurses came to the door to enter. She started yelling: "No, No, No!" She put her hand up and ducked back like in a defensive position.

OMG, what happened to my mom overnight? It got so bad that she would not let them come near her to change her or her bed. She just kept yelling: "No, No, No!" We tried to calm her over the video, but it was not working. The only thing that calmed her was when they left. That night, our lives began to change forever. A new set of nurses came on at 7 p.m. My mom was still upset and did not want them to come near her or touch her. My sister, my uncle, and I begged her to let them change her. That was not like my mom; she loved to be clean and never wanted to go unchanged or uncleaned.

Something was wrong, and it was getting late. I wanted to make sure, while we were on video and could see what was happening, that my mom was all set for the night. I prayed. I hoped that she would hear our voices and that they would give her the comfort and security she needed. It was not working until Nana babies, my mom's grandchildren, got on the video. I remember Nana babies saying: "Come on, Nana, let them change you. You can do this; you got this, Nana."

My sister's kids must have heard us on the phone. They jumped right into the video call. Kids are stronger than we think and so powerful. My mom, their Nana, heard and received them. She gave in. I remember saying: "Thank you, Lord, thank you, Ma."

I just thanked her. She felt and heard her babies. She laid flat in her bed, and they put the head of the bed down. They rolled her from one side to the other side while cleaning her. They changed her gown, had her lay flat, and then it happened so quickly and smoothly—it seemed so seamless—that I questioned myself.

When they raised the bedrails, I saw a pull of something white, and the bed rail went up almost uniformly. One motion, then it was like the phone fell over. My mom was disconnected from the video call.

My uncle said: "Did they just restrain her?"

I was confused and tried to process why they would restrain her.

I said: "They shouldn't have, but I know what we saw." I was mad and scared for my mom. I immediately called back, but there was no answer. We tried again and again, at least four or five times, with no answer. *What was going on?* We were worried.

Shortly after we called back again, they answered the phone. They had my mom's bed in a sitting-up position, and we had a side view. My mom's face was scrunched up; her arms looked stiff beside her.

My first words were: "Is my mother restrained?"

The nurse said: "Yes. I'm the charge nurse." I will refer to her as Nurse X, the "slayer." "She tried to pull her oxygen out of her nose," Nurse X continued.

I was furious. I asked: "At what point in time did she try to pull her oxygen out? We were on the phone when you restrained her before the phone got disconnected when she was not doing anything but lying flat on her back."

Nurse X, the slayer, was very arrogant, reciting like she was reading a textbook, the hospital's protocol about patient safety.

I asked again, trying to rephrase: "At what point did my mother try to pull the oxygen out of her nose? She was already restrained. My mother did not once put her hands up to her face or her nose."

Nurse X, the slayer, never answered my question. She repeated the same thing. Then, Nurse X informed us again that she was the charge nurse and that she had been in the room with my mom for a while. Then she sarcastically stated: "Maybe you need to speak to the provider to get a family member here." I said: "That is exactly what we have been trying to do."

I asked her to have the provider on-call, and the nurse supervisor give me a call. I knew we did not have much time left on the phone. I was trying to assure my mom that she would be okay, but without saying it.

I can still hear my mom say: "It's not okay." From her tone and her demeanor, I did not understand what she meant at that time. But I do now. We were her strength. We had to be strong for her. Even though the odds seemed to be against us, we had to keep praying and keep hope alive, knowing and believing it would be okay.

The nursing supervisor called back. I told her that I was upset and told her of the many complaints, from my mom not being able to listen to her gospel music, being unable to connect with us by video frequently, and an undocumented bruise on the right side of my mom's chest. Then I told her that what finally sent me over the edge was the unexplained use of restraints they placed on my mom when she was lying flat on her back, not doing anything. The nursing supervisor recited the same safety protocol. Clearly, they were all in this together. I asked a clear question. My mom was not doing anything. Why was she restrained? The nursing supervisor did not respond to the question that I had asked. I said that I understood the safety protocol, but she was not doing anything but lying there on her back. What had she done that put her safety at risk, and that required that she be restrained? No one answered my question, and the nursing supervisor told me she would pass all of my concerns over to the nurse manager in the morning.

Then, the on-call provider called. She was ready for me. She was already irritated. I heard it in her voice, and I asked the same question. Still, to this day, I have not gotten an answer to justify the restraints. I spoke slowly and clearly to be sure there would be no miscommunication or misunderstanding about what I was asking.

Since I wasn't getting anywhere there, I asked if my mom was sedated. The on-call provider was quick to tell me that they gave her a psychotic medicine to calm her down. Long story short, they sedated her due to the paralyzing effect I told everyone those antipsychotic medications have on my mom. And that was how they were using them, as sedation. Before the on-call provider had called, I had checked my mom's labs through her health portal app. I was concerned about some of her results; some were high, some were low. Her recent results, again as I Googled them, led me back to hypoxia. They were consistent with hypoxia; the causes and symptoms of hypoxia seemed to match exactly my mom's symptoms.

I asked the on-call provider about the labs, and she informed me that my mom's main provider, who is Provider 2, would be there during the day and that I needed to talk to him about the bloodwork. I was confused. She was the on-call provider. She called me back about my concerns, and she refused to answer any of my questions. *What is her job, and what does she do? What happened to the communication?* I was supposed to be notified of any change with my mom. It had always been that way, until now.

I spent a lot of time talking to the Lord that night, begging, pleading. "Please look over my mom, protect her, give her the strength she needs to get through this day. God, please help us get my mom to a safe environment." It had to be about 1 a.m. I remember telling my sister: "The next shift comes on at 7 a.m. We have to make it through the next six hours."

I thought to myself: *Six hours is a very long time. I have faith.* I was up, talking to the Lord. Talking to my mom in my head, letting her know I love her, and please hang in there. I couldn't sleep, I cried. The next morning, April 12, 2021, I tried several times to get in touch with her nurse. I needed to make sure my mom was okay. When I finally reached her nurse, I asked how my mom was doing and if she was sedated. The nurse said they did have to sedate her that morning. When I asked why the nurse informed me that my mom would not take her medication.

My voice was shaking. "You have got to be kidding me. You mean to tell me you sedated my mother because she would not take her medication?" I asked her to page Provider 2 to give me a call. Again, I called patient relations that same day very upset, and I filed yet another complaint. They sedated my mom for not taking her medicine and restrained her when she was not doing anything but lying on her back. This was totally unacceptable. I told him I intended to call the Health Department and the Joint Commission on Accreditation of Health Care Organizations (JCAHO) to complain. I asked patient relations how to get copies of all of the correspondence and complaints that I had filed. He informed me that I could not get these documents. I asked if my lawyer, the state, and so on would be able to get a copy. He said yes.

I Googled and called lawyers in the area, but I could speak only with an intake person. I told the intake person at each lawyer's office my situation. At the end of the call, each of them told me that the lawyers were unable to take the case. This happened time after time. I surfed the Internet, and I found numbers for the JCAHO and the Health Department. I don't remember which was which, but I was told by one of them that I had to fill out a form online. The other one informed me they could not do anything while the patient was still admitted; she had to be discharged for them to be able to assist me.

For years, I had heard about all these policies that help and protect patients. Where was my mom's help? The system had failed her. I called the NAACP, which was working remotely due to COVID-19, and a woman called me back. After I explained the situation, she told me that they do not have lawyers and that they were not able to help. She did tell me who to write to. It was frustrating, but we kept praying.

Everyone knows that when my mom gets upset or uses too much energy, her oxygen drops, and she becomes short of breath. I had not been able to video call with her. I got so many excuses like something was wrong with her phone, her phone charger was broken, and they didn't have a phone to do a video call with. They were a year into a pandemic. They should have learned by then how to keep the families connected.

Provider 2, my mom's main provider on the PCU floor, called. I started by telling him I was very upset. My voice was still shaking. I described the chain of events, how I called the nurse to see how my mom was doing and asked if she was se-dated. The nurse had the nerve, the audacity, to tell me that she had sedated my mom because my mom did not want to take her medication. Shame on the nurse. Provider 2 told me that maybe the nurse misspoke.

I replied: "Misspoke? No, she meant what she said. I repeated it back to the nurse. There was no misspeaking. The nurse also informed me she was still restrained. Shame on you." I told him that they restrained my mom overnight while she was lying flat on her back in bed, not doing anything. They said it was because she tried to pull her oxygen out of her nose. We were on video and saw that she was restrained for no reason. Before the call disconnected, I said: "You are my mom's main provider; you, as well as all the others, are responsible for my mom's care and safety." Again, I asked about my mom's blood work, still concerned about blood clots and hypoxia. I was still not getting anywhere in mentioning it to the provider. Not being able to help my mom was so frustrating. The different events that took place that week were on his watch, in his hands. I was pissed.

I was overcome with sarcasm. I told him: "Thank you for being there for our family when we could not be there due to COVID-19. Thank you because you were the only ones who could have helped, but you chose not to. Thank you for failing us." When I asked about my mom's transfer status, he said that she was still waiting on an ICU step-down bed.

The nightmare was never-ending. I thought there was a whistleblower non-retaliation policy that protects the patient. The system failed in the middle of an active pandemic when we needed the system the most.

Chapter 7

Remember the charge nurse, Nurse X, the slayer, from the night before, who restrained my mom for nothing when she was lying on her back? She was one of the ones I had a complaint against. I believe Nurse X played a huge part in my mom's change in status. What are the chances that Nurse X, previously the charge nurse, was now my mom's nurse on April 12, 2021, at 7 p.m. for the next twelve hours? Filing complaints and trying to help my mom only brought her torture and retaliation.

It made me wonder, and I can only speak for this hospital, whether they received a stipend for the COVID-19 patients whom they let die, helped to die, or caused to be put on a ventilator. This hospital had proven to me that it would go above and beyond to make sure it happens. I saw the wrong, but I had to humble myself and stop filing complaints. At least at that point, or I thought there was a good chance my mom would not make it out of there alive. I was scared for my mom's life, with no one to call and no one to help. The system failed.

Not being able to video chat with my mom was painful; my heart was troubled. Then I got a call from the irritated on-call provider from the previous night, the one in cahoots with Nurse X, about restraining my mom for nothing. Someone must have said something because now the communication was back. She informed me that my mom required more oxygen and that she wouldn't keep her oxygen in her nose. She was combative, and her oxygen dropped into the sixties due to her pulling her oxygen out.

I was thinking: *This isn't good. Humble yourself; this is your mother's life.* I asked if my mom was sedated and was told that the order says continuously as needed. I called the nursing station to have the charge nurse call me back so that I could get connected with my mom. The charge nurse called back.

I was asking how to get a video call going with my mom, and the charge nurse was quick to give me an update. It was the same as the on-call provider. Mom required more oxygen, but she pulled her oxygen out of her nose. Then she said that my mom's oxygen had dropped into the thirties.

"What are you talking about?" I asked. "I just spoke to the on-call provider. She stated it dropped into the sixties." Even then, I knew the sixties were bad.

The charge nurse sarcastically said: "Uh, it may have been in the sixties when the on-call provider saw it. When we were in there, she dropped into the thirties."

Was she boasting? There was nothing I could do, as my mom still could not have visitors. My heart was broken. I called my sister, bawling. It was so sad. I felt helpless. My sister and I went over the chain of events, but nothing was making sense.

How could they sedate my mom when she did not take her medicine, but they did not sedate her when she supposedly pulled her oxygen out of her nose, with them in the room, and they saw and let her oxygen drop to the thirties? What happened to the hospital's patient safety protocol? Around 5 a.m. on April 13, 2021, with two hours left in her shift, I got a call from Nurse X, the slayer, who asked if I wanted to talk to my mom.

I said: "I want to see my mom."

Nurse X called me on a video call. She was holding the phone on herself and trying to give me an update. I said: "I want to see my mother." Nurse X turned the phone to my mom, then turned it back to herself. I still had a glimpse of my mom due to the way she held the phone. My mom looked pissed. Not sedated, not zoned out, just pissed. I could see that she was still restrained.

Nurse X went on to tell me that my mom was restrained for trying to pull her oxygen out of her nose. According to Nurse X, the slayer, my mom bent one of the nurse's fingers, twisted one of their wrists, and ripped off one of their gowns, which was supposed to protect the staff from COVID-19. And she spit on one of them.

I said: "Wait a minute. You mean to tell me that my mom bent a finger, twisted a wrist, ripped off a gown, and spit on someone, all while she was restrained?"

Incredibly, Nurse X said, "yes."

I was thinking: *Really?* You know her story: *Her phlegm is so thick it chokes her to bring it up. But she was able to spit on someone?*

I still had my mother insight, and my mom yelled: **"She pulled it out of my nose!"** She was clear as day, not slurred or anything. My hair stood up. I will never forget that. Now, I know that a leopard cannot change its spots. Of course, Nurse X, the slayer, heard it. She was right there. She was the one holding the phone, and she didn't try to justify it. She didn't say anything.

I know that what I did and said next was very important. In my head, I was having a woosah moment. *My mother's life depends on this, regroup.* I asked: "Can I see my mom?"

Nurse X, the slayer, held the phone on my mom and didn't leave the room. We had never had a video call with someone holding the phone or remaining in the room. I looked into my mother's eyes. She was pissed off. Her face was scrunched up, her eyes were squinted, and her mouth was tightly closed. I could see the fumes coming from her. Looking into her eyes, I told her: "I love you, I heard you, I will take care of it, I promise." It took everything in me to hold it together and be strong for my mom. I could not be there at the hospital with my mom because of the policy.

After the call was over, I asked the Lord to please watch over her, protect her, humble her soul, and humble my soul. I called my sister, so upset, and I told her: "Mom yelled clearly, 'She pulled it out of my nose,' referring to Nurse X." I will never ever forget that. You reap what you sow, Lord, help us. They are trying to kill my mom. I can only speak for this hospital. I thought providers and nurses took the Hippocratic oath to do no harm, but not at this hospital.

In the middle of a pandemic, did this hospital become stipend over patient care? My mind wondered. Earlier, my mom had a horrible look of fear that something had happened to her. Please remember, they said my mom bent a finger, twisted a wrist, pulled a gown off, and spit on someone, all while she was restrained. It's hard to envision how these events could have occurred, but if they did, I am not trying to justify them. But they must have been doing something awfully bad to my mom so that she felt that her life was in jeopardy and that she had to fight like her life depended on it while in restraints.

Chapter 8

On April 13, 2021, at around noon, I received a call from the nursing coordinator about an emergency zoom meeting at 2 p.m. that day to go over my concerns. She informed me that the whole medical team would be there, including the providers and the psychiatrist. I informed the nurse coordinator that my sister had an appointment at that time and that this was short notice. I was basically informed that it was then or never. The provider, the nurse coordinator, the psychiatrist, and I were on the zoom call. I could see on the zoom attending list that my sister was trying to connect during her appointment, but she was unable to.

We all introduced ourselves. The nurse coordinator had me start the conversation. I remembered that, to my knowledge, this was an emergency meeting about my concerns with my mom's care. I had just filed another complaint yesterday with patient relations and let them know I was calling the Health Department and JCAHO to file a complaint. Now the hospital came up with this emergency zoom meeting. I started with the unexplained bruise on my mom's chest. The nurse coordinator quickly jumped in, letting me know they were on a tight time schedule, and we have a lot to cover. We moved on, but not before the nurse coordinator sarcastically asked how I saw a bruise on my mom's chest when she was not letting anyone come near her. I informed the nurse coordinator the fear that my mom had just shown was after something had taken place that I was unaware of. Before she developed the fear, I was on a video call with her nurse. My mom was unable to speak at the time due to the medicine and what was going on with her. But I know that she sat straight up to show me the bruise. The top of her gown fell down. There was the bruised sore with a scab on it clear as day. I told the nurse coordinator that I took a picture of it. Nothing else was said about it. They moved on.

I felt like this hospital was trying to cover its tracks and justify the unjustifiable continuous use of restraints and sedation on my mom. Ask me how? By painting this picture of my mom on the zoom call as being violent and abusive towards the staff. We all remember the story they told the day before regarding her bending a finger, twisting a wrist, and so on while she was restrained. My mom had been at this hospital for one month and a few days. At no point in time did anyone ever mention or categorize my mom as being violent or abusive until yesterday, when they were informed that I was calling the state. I think they realized at this point that the family knew, saw, and witnessed too much. That was why the nurse coordinator said that moving forward, we, the family, could possibly only have one call a day at a certain time. The nurse coordinator stated that it was because my mom needed her privacy and that she needs to be able to rest.

Let's do a recap.

Within the first month of my mom's hospital admission, she went into delirium and a state of confusion. The provider at that time was amazed by my mom's turnaround and progress coming out of delirium. The provider informed me it was because of us, the family being there on the video talking and engaging her in conversation. That is what brought her out of a state of confusion. The provider also stated the hospital tries to keep patients out of delirium, but they do not have the staff or time that is required.

My understanding of the new treatment plan that would help my mom's condition was organized by the nurse coordinator. Per the nurse coordinator, the treatment plan was as follows; One possible video call a day with family because my mom needed her privacy and rest.

I did not think about this until later, but I asked myself how would this help my mom and her delirium? If the hospital could not keep her out of her current state of confusion, while they were going into her room every two hours, twenty-four hours a day, seven days a week, what makes them think one possible video call with family would be enough to help bring her out of delirium? I wonder was this new treatment plan based on my mom's medical condition or what I stated earlier; this hospital realized the family knew, saw, and witnessed too much. My mom was unable to speak; she needed family, not separation from us that was not going to help her.

As the meeting went on, I started to block them out. I realized that this meeting had nothing to do with me or my concerns about my mom's care. I did ask about the status of my mom's transfer. The nurse coordinator sternly and quickly answered that mom would not be leaving this hospital. I remember how quickly I frowned. I pulled my head back like what? The provider quickly jumped in and tried to correct and smooth out what she meant. I couldn't say anything because I was shocked and confused because this nurse coordinator was confident that my mom was not leaving. I had a sense of fear for my mom. Did the nurse coordinator know something that I did not?

It was a continuous nightmare that I couldn't wake up from. The same evening of the emergency zoom meeting, I received a call from a provider saying that my mom required more oxygen and that they had moved her to the ICU. This wasn't good. All I could hear was: "She pulled it out of my nose."

I was proactive, and I had been in contact with the receiving hospital that I wanted my mom to be transferred to, telling them my concerns and checking on her bed status for myself. I was panicking. I explained to them, again, that if my mom did not get out of this hospital soon, I knew that she wouldn't make it out of there alive. The receiving hospital informed me that a bed was available, and they sent the paperwork over to the facility where my mom was and let them know about the available bed on April 13, 2021, at around 5 p.m.

Please follow me on this. I received the call from the provider at about 6 p.m. The provider knew when he called me that my mom had a bed at the other hospital and was ready for transfer.

He did not let me know. I had a flashback. Earlier, during the emergency zoom meeting, when I asked about my mom's transfer, the nurse coordinator told me sternly that my mom would not be leaving this hospital. Those were her exact words. I did not understand at that time what she meant. But now I understood that she meant it literally. This hospital would go to any extreme to keep my mom there, even putting her life in jeopardy to stop her transfer.

I gave an update to the receiving hospital to see the likelihood of my mom getting transferred now that she required more oxygen and is in ICU. Basically, the process would start over, and the provider would have to send an update. She had to go back on the waitlist now for an ICU bed. I said: "So, it is still a possibility she would be able to transfer?"

The person said: "Yes, she should be able to, as long as there is no tubing or intubation."

My heart felt like it stopped. I felt sick to my stomach, numb. If this hospital kept to its usual pattern, I was heartbroken over the thought of what would happen next. I knew this hospital's next move. I felt there was nothing I could do to stop it. I prayed that it was not true.

Chapter 9

I must have fallen asleep waiting. I sat straight up in the bed, frantic, soaking wet. I was trying to find my bearings, grasping my surroundings, telling myself, *It's okay*, and *I'm okay*. I calmed myself a little and went into the living room. I didn't go anywhere in those days without my phone. My phone rang, and my heart dropped. Please continue to follow me here. Late-night into the early morning, the same night as the emergency zoom meeting, I received that anticipated call from the provider.

He was calling about my mom, and I connected my sister on the line. The provider informed us that my mom required more oxygen. They had to intubate her. My Lord! We were concerned, scared, and asking questions. The conversation went on for a little bit, and right before the provider was about to end the conversation, he said: "We had to put her on a ventilator."

Painful. What kind of closing remark was that? I told him: "The whole time we were on the phone, asking questions, you heard our concerns. You spoke only of intubation. You didn't think that it was important to let us know our mom was on a ventilator? You could have started with that earlier."

My fear was now a reality, and I was upset, angry, and hurt. I called the accepting hospital, bawling, and informed them what had happened. *Who would have known?* Ten minutes earlier, I had sat straight up, soaking wet, frantic, and I knew: my mom was being put on a ventilator. She didn't use her mouth to tell me. She connected with my mind. I felt it.

The ICU provider called and told us that— listen to this— "Your mom is suffering from hypoxia, a lack of oxygen. That is where her confusion, disorientation, and combativeness probably came from, and"—brace for this— "she has two blood clots, one in her leg and one in her lungs. That would explain the increasing need for more oxygen and shortness of breath. Also, she has a new injury to her kidney that may be due to the medications."

Jesus, take the wheel. I was numb. I had told Provider 2 and previously spoke many times of my suspicion that my mom was experiencing hypoxia and blood clots, just from Googling her lab results, but because I don't have MD after my name, I guess I was not smart enough. What he was really telling us was that our mom was sedated, restrained, tortured, used, abused, and neglected because this hospital misdiagnosed her. She went through hell, and I could only imagine a fragment of the pain and suffering she endured and of what we saw. And there was more that the ICU provider had the nerve to say. They would be working on getting my mom COVID cleared. She was past the COVID-19 guidelines. They would be in contact with infectious diseases, then start the decontamination process so that my mom could have visitors.

Was this all to say *we did a whole hell of a lot of wrong things, and now we need to do our job and try to rectify them?* Hopefully, the family would be so caught up in the moment that they would forget all of this hospital's wrongdoing, and it would just go away. My feelings were flooding like a dam that had broken. I was happy, sad, mad, hurt, pissed off, confused, and grateful. My mom had been in this hospital for thirty-plus days; everyone knew she was past the COVID-19 guidelines. Still, they never allowed family there. I thanked the provider and asked him about the likelihood of a safe transfer for my mom since she was on a ventilator with two blood clots. He informed me that it was possible. I asked what the team would look like that would be transporting her. Would there be a respiratory therapist and a provider on board? He responded that neither a respiratory therapist nor a provider would be accompanying my mom during the transfer. I asked how we could secure a provider and a respiratory therapist to assist in the transfer, but this was not an option.

The next day, April 15, 2021, I received a call that they were starting the decontamination process, then my mom could have visitors. Everything happened so fast. I then received another call saying that my mom was breathing at 90-some percent on her own. They were going to watch her for a while and then extubate. That was a lot, and I was processing a little slower. I was again confused, happy, grateful, and concerned. I voiced my concerns to the provider.

"I am so glad my mom is doing well and breathing on her own. But is she really ready? Is it too soon? After a day and a half, her struggle is now over? She just started the medication for blood clots a day and a half ago. Was that enough time for the medicine to get in her system and work? And she would not require more and more oxygen, like what she did to end up on a ventilator this time?" We loved our mom and wanted what was best for her and for her to be okay. I received a call from the nurse around noon the same day telling me that they just extubated my mom and had taken her off the ventilator. Her nurse did a video call with me; it was a beautiful thing, looking back.

It was like a baby being born. It was beautiful; even though she was swollen and looked exhausted, her eyes were barely open, and they were suctioning her out. I was coaching her as she coughed: "You can do it, get that stuff out of you." I was so excited. She was beautiful, and she could hear and see me. By that evening, she could have visitors, someone was there by her side, and we made sure that every day after that, the family was there.

Chapter 10

Legally, my sister and I were Mom's healthcare representatives, making all of her healthcare decisions per our mom at the beginning of her stay. It was a breath of fresh air, knowing that a family member could be with my mom. I remember my sister saying that they seemed a little better on this floor, but she did not trust them. Remember, we still needed to transfer mom.

The nurse said that my mom had a flag or note on her chart about being violent. The nurse could not believe it, as she said that my mom was a sweetheart. It was probably the hypoxia causing that.

I live in another state, and I had been managing my mom's care over the phone. My mom having visitors before then was not an option. According to the hospital, before then, she had to be at the end of her life before she could have visitors. I stayed put until the Lord told me that it was time to move. I will never forget it; we were still embracing and rejoicing about the milestones we had reached in two days.

On April 17, 2021, at around 8:55 in the morning, I was at work when I received a phone call. It was a provider at the hospital informing me that my mom's status had changed. They had spoken to my mom. She wanted to be changed to Do Not Resuscitate (DNR). She was aware of what that meant; she would pass on.

"Stop! My mom is not a DNR. How could you override her legal documents, and if this is the end of life, the family is supposed to have the opportunity to be there." I told him I was on my way, and I asked when the rest of the family could come. He said he would check and call me back. I called my sister to let her know what was going on, and for her to get to the hospital as quickly as possible, I was on my way.

The Lord told me that it was time to move. I knew for sure that this hospital was trying to kill my mom. About two hours later, I received a call from the same provider stating that my mom's condition remained unchanged and that the hospital policy stands: only one visitor a day. *Can someone help me? Two hours ago, I got a phone call stating my mom was taking her last breath, and now two hours later, she was not.* I was told earlier by the provider that, if ever my mom got to an end-of-life status, her family would be able to be by her side. When I was told she was taking her last breath, to me, that meant end-of-life. I asked about family being there by her side. Then, I was informed that she was not taking her last breath, and her status was unchanged. We were riding an emotional rollercoaster.

My sister arrived at the hospital, and we did a video call before I boarded the plane. I let my mom know that I was on my way.

Chapter 11

The next morning, April 18, 2021, I was at the hospital from 8 a.m. to 8 p.m. When I arrived, I was so excited. I had made it there, and she was still breathing. When I got to her door, she was getting her mouth cleaned out, and she saw me. I saw the excitement, too, and I threw up my hands. "Thank you, Lord, I'm here. I'm here, Ma."

She started laughing. I saw a tear. I will hold that sight close to my heart always. I went beside her bed. "Hello, beautiful." I rubbed her head, I kissed her, and said, "I love you." I told her I was going to put on her favorite gospel music. The providers, a team of about five, were rounding outside her door. The nurse informed me I could stand in on the update. I went outside my mom's door and introduced myself. They went over her labs and everything. I stood in every day after that. They asked if I had any questions. I asked what the status of my mom's transfer was. The provider, whom I will call Provider 3, said that he would check into it and get back to me, and I went back into my mom's room. I had just met her nurse before the provider did rounds. The nurse was a bit cocky and overconfident. She came back into the room like someone had sent her to pry after being in the hallway with the providers.

She sat on the rolling stool and slid herself over to my mom's bed. She said: "I never got to ask you why you want to transfer your mother to another hospital."

Wait in my head again, I just met her, and what business is it of hers? These nurses sure do not know their place. Who does she think she is to question me? Most importantly, who does she think I am, stupid? Knowing that this facility was trying to eliminate my mom, and it would be considered due to COVID-19? Each floor brought something different to the table, like there were different phases to the process. I said that her primary care provider and regular team of providers are over there. This hospital took my mom off the ventilator after she was on it for only a day and a half, then two days later, this hospital said that my mom was taking her last breath. Yet, she was still alive. I remember when my mom said: "You do not see what's going on right in front of you?" I saw it now.

I wanted to check my mother's foot, as we were concerned about it on a video call. When she could not have visitors, I mentioned it to Provider 2, who informed us that he did not see any darkness or swelling in either of her feet. Maybe it was the lighting. I wanted to check her foot for myself since she had diabetes. Lo and behold, it was dark like we saw in the video. Why would Provider 2 lie? I mentioned my concern to the nurse. She felt my mom's foot and said it was okay since it had a pulse.

I made every effort to keep the same routine, putting on her gospel music, cleaning and disinfecting her room, talking to her to lift her spirits, washing her face, cleaning her mouth, combing her hair, and moisturizing her lips, all to let her keep her dignity. It was amazing after I arrived on April 18, 2021; within two days, the family was doing video calls and sing-alongs with my mom. Some days, my mom could talk and sing; some days, she could not. We had some good days. The bad days were really bad. I stayed with my mom from 8 a.m. to 8 p.m. I did not eat, drink, leave her room, or use the bathroom. My primary concern was to let her catch up on her well-deserved rest. She knew that she could sleep easily, as no one was going to do anything to her with her family there. I constantly cleaned her room. The negligence I saw was sad. I was keeping a mental note. Some things may seem small, but all were important to my mom's health. Some things you cannot teach in a school like friendliness, kindness, common sense, caring, compassion, and empathy. These characteristics have to be in you already.

I brought her brother in from out-of-town on April 21, 2021, to visit for a day and to keep an eye on her. He kept the same routine with my mom so that I could have a chance to regroup and replay the different incidents. I came back the next day excited to see my mom. I asked if she enjoyed her visit with her brother, all the singing and video calls they did. She asked me was he here. I realized at that moment she did not remember. I quickly changed the conversation. It was bitter-sweet. Later, I informed the family. The things my mom had endured, maybe this was not the time for her to be burdened with remembering them. No one should have to relive it. We prayed that it was not permanent. I looked around the room; you know how I feel about her routine. The disposable suction tube used to suction out her mouth was filthy. There had to be a protocol for changing them. I spent a lot of time observing before I spoke. The nurse came in and changed her and the bed. During the process, the suction tube hit the floor. They hung it up on the wall hook. Once they finished and everything was said and done, they put the mouth suction back on the bed for her to use.

I said: "It fell on the floor. Do you see how filthy it is with all the build-up in it? She needs a new one; when do you change them?" I asked: "Could we please make sure she has a clean suction tube daily? The nurse looked at the mouth suction as she was disconnecting it." Her only response was that she would get a new one. I said: "Act like this is your mom in this bed. What would you do?" There was no response again from the nurse, who seemed irritated that I had asked. During one of these times, they got my mom out of the bed and into the chair by using a Hoyer lift and a fabric seat that stayed under her. She had an accident in the chair. They came and cleaned her up. I watched to make sure everything was disinfected. I remember it clear as day. There was a foldable, plastic, wipeable seat cushion, and a little accident got on it. The nurse picked it up and glanced at it. I saw it, and I know that she saw it. She still folded the cushion and put it up in my mom's cabinet. *Lazy and nasty, doesn't she know about germs and infections that patients can catch, or does she even care? What do they do when the family is not there?* When they left, I disinfected my mom's whole room, rails, cushion, cabinet, and all.

I was attentive to my mom. A nurse came in to give her insulin. I must have blinked my eyes. I heard my mom scream, and I asked what happened. The nurse told me he gave her insulin. I asked: "Where did you give it?"

He said: "In her leg."

Who gives insulin in the leg? I asked him to make a note in her chart: Do not ever give my mom insulin in her legs; it is too painful.

They were constantly making changes to her insulin. I couldn't understand the first floor my mom was admitted to. Her sugar levels were high and low. But they knew how to regulate them. But, during the latter part of her stay, they didn't know what they were doing. Once, there was a problem with her insulin dose. The nurse talked to the provider, whom I will call Provider 4, and they went back and forth. The nurse disagreed with Provider 4, and it seemed like the nurses were above the providers at times. The nurse left the room, and I heard her speaking to someone in the hall. When she came back into the room, I asked: "What's going on with my mom's insulin?" What she said made sense of everything. She told me that these students, residents, think they know everything. She went and spoke to; I think she said, the fellow provider to get the correct insulin dose.

I asked: "Are all these providers and nurses here students, fresh out of school residents, and so on?"

She said most of them. She's a nurse, and there were more nurses on. I said they should not be on this floor. She said: "Well, they have to learn."

I said: "Yes, but not in the ICU, where patients are very critical and could die because of their negligence." I knew this was a teaching hospital, but I thought that they would not teach in the ICU.

My mom was getting insulin so often that she became sore and sensitive. One nurse came to give her insulin in the fatty back part of her arm, and mom didn't flinch. I asked the nurse if she could note that the fatty back part of her arm is a good place to give her insulin so that my mom's stomach, where they had been giving her insulin, could get a break. I thought that everything was okay. A day passed, and I went to lotion my mom's arms. *What in the world?* It looked like they went to war with my mom's arms. I said to give her insulin in the fatty back part of her arm, not her major muscles. She is not a training mannequin. She's human, and she's breathing; she feels pain just like you. I was constantly telling them: "Act like this is your mom in this bed. What would you do?" I always mentioned that to them in the hope that they would not repeat their actions.

I brought in pictures of my mom before her hospital stay with her and our family. I put them on her wall, so I was frequently having the act-like-this-is-your-mom conversation. I even started taking a picture off the wall, bringing it to her bedside, showing them, and telling them not to judge or look at my mom in her current physical form. I made a circle with my hands around my mom in bed and the picture. "This is my mother. Who suffers? My mom, the patient."

We desperately need a bed to become available at the other facility. When the nurse came to draw blood, she went to stick my mom in her arm. The seasoned nurse came behind her and asked what she was doing and told the nurse to draw blood from the IV. I guess she was a student or fresh out of school. We should always do what is best for the patient.

My mom's arms were black and purple. "My mom has been in this hospital almost a month and a half, drawing blood every day, throughout the day. Save her some pain. Who suffers? My mom, the patient." The students should never be unsupervised.

On another occasion, as they were changing my mom, she was moaning and screaming in pain. A seasoned nurse said it was due to the catheter, as they were cleaning around it. I went over to my mom's bedside because it sounded painful. I saw exactly why she was screaming. I said: "Do you not see? She has no skin on her inner thighs."

The wounds on both sides of her inner thighs were bigger than my hands opened wide. I said: "Act like this is your mother lying here. What would you do?" I apologized to my mom for not stepping in sooner. "Why did they lie? Who suffers? My mom, the patient. I asked them to call Provider 3 to put in an order for cream or something to help.

On another occasion, a nurse came to give my mom her breathing treatment. The nurse was about to change her oxygen mask. I asked her: "Why don't you do what the other nurses do to make it easier on my mom? They put the albuterol medicine in that bubble attachment and use the same mask, so it does not pull at her feeding tube." She said: "One moment and left the room." I wondered if she was a nurse in training or fresh out of school. She came back in and said, "Okay," and then she started to pour the liquid treatment into the empty space. I told her again: "There is an attachment."

She said that she had spoken with her charge nurse, who told her it goes right in. I could see the little bit that she poured running down the tube. That other nurse was right. The students don't listen. The seasoned nurse came in, got the bubble attachment, and poured the medicine into it. That's what unsupervised help will get you. Who suffers? My mom, the patient.

I repeatedly asked: "Please be careful around my mom's face." I witnessed her feeding tube being yanked on multiple occasions while changing her, rotating her, and so on. I can only imagine how painful it was because of her screams.

Aside from the nurses having no empathy or compassion, they also were detached. When I was younger, my mom would say: "It goes in one ear and out the other."

Chapter 12

I left at 8 p.m. one night and went to my sister's home to get settled. At about 10 p.m., I received a call from a provider who said that my mom was a DNR. I was freaking out about what happened, as I had just left. I connected my sister on the line, and the provider repeated that she was a DNR, and they needed me to sign the paperwork. I said: "You have no bedside manners, calling me at 10 p.m., which would cause alarm, just for some paperwork. My mother is not a DNR, and we are not signing anything." It seemed like they were trying to tag team me.

The next night, I received a call from Provider 4, who gave me an update and basically let me know that my mom was not following commands. Provider 4 said that she had been like that with them for a few days.

They were giving her more antipsychotic (sedation) drugs to try to clear her mind and to see if she would come around. I informed him that, while I was at the hospital that day, I got her to squeeze my hand and nod her head. I also informed him that the medication was only sedating her.

Provider 4 replied that sometimes families want to believe that their family members are getting better or doing certain things. But, until she shows them, she is listed as not following commands. *Is he calling me a liar?*

That next morning, Provider 3, the main provider on the ICU floor, came into the room to check on my mom, but it was really to have the DNR conversation with me. I was standing at the foot of my mom's bed, and we were listening to her gospel music. Provider 3 stood beside me. We were both looking at my mom when he asked if I had thought about signing the DNR papers.

I told him that my mom didn't tell me she wanted to be a DNR. "Until she does, nothing changes."

Provider 3 stated: "She told us."

I said: "Who is us?"

He said he was there.

I turned to him and said: "No disrespect, Doc, but until my mother tells me, I'm not signing."

He asked: "Could we try to have that conversation with her now?"

I said: "I thought you had to be alert and oriented. My mother is currently not speaking."

Provider 3 said: "It looks like you would want to honor your mother's wishes."

I told him: "I know what my mom's wishes are, and I am not signing."

Provider 3 said that we would want to know the plan. "The time is almost near."

I said: "Only God knows."

Provider 3 said that since I would not honor my mother's wishes, he would remove the DNR order and change her status. I asked again about the status of her transfer. He informed me that he would have case management call, and he left.

I kept replaying what he said: *The time is almost near." What does he mean? How was he so confident? "The time is almost near?"*

I was thinking, *we all must die. Still, we don't know the day or the hour.* Provider 3 was so confident and arrogant: *"The time was almost near."* My mind wandered, and I asked myself: *Was his confidence that her time was almost near, because he is the provider, and he knew the pain and suffering that they had inflicted on her, mixed with the right combinations of medications that he knew would and did cause more damage to her already damaged organs? Were they constantly sedating her so that she would be unable to speak about the torture they had inflicted, constantly restraining her for a health condition they failed to treat? Or was it because COVID-19 has been here for a year, and he— I can only speak about this provider—and this hospital had their fair share of COVID-19 patients to test and experiment on, and now this hospital knew exactly what to do, and how to kill or help kill her faster, and her death would be due to COVID-19? He has been doing this for so long that he thinks he is God.*

It seemed to me that he knew when my mom would die. As I thought about it if that was the case, why did he not have that conversation with me? What happened to my mom's right to have family members by her bedside? I opened my mom's sliding glass doors, and the nurse was there.

I asked: "Can you page Provider 3 to come back?" Then I asked: "What did he mean? 'The time is almost near.' Like my mom is dying, and no one yet has said that to me."

The nurse said: "No, he didn't mean it like that. He was saying we need to have a plan in place."

In my head, I thought: *This is crazy; how did the nurse know the answer to my question? She was not in the room.* Then I remembered what my mom had said earlier: "They are listening?" Maybe she was just expressing her opinion about what Provider 3 had meant.

Case management called me promptly and introduced herself. She was also the manager of case management. She would be the one taking over my mom's case and would be the main contact person. I asked her about the transfer, and she informed me that they were working on it. Then she asked if I was aware that we may have to pay for the ambulance ride because the insurance company may deny the transfer due to our request to have her transferred to another hospital. I said that we had been informed earlier by someone and that it was not a problem. She said she just wanted to let me know, as we may have to sign a waiver. I let her know we were prepared to sign and do whatever else was necessary. That was the end of my first call with the case manager.

A few minutes later, she called back to let me know there could be a cost for the accepting hospital. They were working on the authorization, but if my mom was transferred before it was approved and the insurance denied it, we may be responsible for the bill, and they may request that we sign a statement acknowledging that we could be responsible. I explained to her that, no matter what the financial responsibilities were, the family was aware and ready to sign, do, and pay whatever was necessary. That was the end of our second conversation.

I received another call from her a few minutes later letting me know that my mother requires a lot of oxygen, and they do not have an ambulance service-equipped to transport her. I said that when she was on a ventilator with higher oxygen requirements, she was to be transferred if a bed became available. What ambulance service did they have then? She said she was checking, and the third conversation ended. I was getting frustrated. *Something is going on. They are up to something.*

Yet another call. She was making sure my mother's paperwork was in order. As it stands, my mother was a DNR. *Here we go again.* That meant that, at this hospital, she would be a DNR, but without the signed papers when she gets transported, her status would become a full code meaning all effects would be made to resuscitate her if needed. There are many risk factors with the transfer and the amount of oxygen required. I said: "It is our hope and prayer that everything goes well with the transfer transport."

Four calls within a forty-minute time frame, and each call was to discourage me from transferring my mom. Shortly after the call, I saw someone rolling what appeared to be a ventilator outside my mom's room. No one had mentioned this to me. I kept her room curtain pulled closed enough that she wouldn't see it.

The next day, while Provider 3 was rounding, he asked if case management had gotten in touch with me. I said yes, and I informed him that we were willing to pay, sign, and do whatever was required for the transfer.

Provider 3 said: "It's not about the money. Your mother is not stable or medically cleared for transfer."

I said: "What are you talking about?" Now follow me here. This is the same Provider I had been speaking to every day about my mom's transfer, and this was unknown to me. Provider 3 then had the nerve to inform me that my mom's transfer had been on hold since she went on the ventilator. I was pissed. Another provider had lied to me. I had been asking every day. No one had ever made mentioned this until that moment. We were always told that we were waiting for a bed.

I did not think about it until later, but if my mom was not stable and medically cleared when I asked him yesterday about the status of her transfer, why did he not inform me then? Why did he contact case management, and why did case management at no point tell me that my mom was not stable or medically cleared for transfer? This was horrible. The great measures they took and would take to keep her there proved that they were determined not to let my mom go.

I believe that my mom was used as an undocumented COVID-19 case study in the middle of an active COVID-19 pandemic. My mother had every major illness in one body. They are a training, teaching hospital, and they could and did learn a lot from her.

Chapter 13

I visited with my mom, and the next day she was again sedated. The providers made rounds, and my mom did not follow any of their commands. I still told her it was okay.

Providers 3 and 4 left, but the nurse was still in the room. I had remembered that my mom wrote a book, and I had picked it up the day before. I went to my backpack to get it. I pulled her book out and showed her. I said: "Look, you did it, Ma. The publisher called yesterday to have your books picked up."

She had so much excitement on her face. Even though she had not spoken for some time, she said: "That's my book."

I said: "Yes."

She kept repeating it. By that time, the nurse and some others were by her bedside. They said: "You wrote a book?"

My mom said, "Yes," talking to them.

You know how you feel someone is watching you? I turned around, and outside my mom's room was Provider 4, who had stated earlier that he knew that sometimes the family wanted to believe that their family member was getting better or doing certain things. He was peeking around the corner, looking at my mom talking.

I told Provider 4: "No, come in." I wanted him to bear witness that the Lord showed up, and my mom showed out. Thank you, Lord. I told Provider 4 that he needed to take her off the sedation. Later, Provider 3 stopped in. He was her main ICU provider, the one who stood with me at the foot of her bed discussing the DNR order this morning, the same provider who told me that my mom was not stable or medically cleared for transfer this same morning. He was standing there now a few hours later, letting me know they were working on her transfer.

My mom was now stable and medically cleared. This was the same day, the same provider. The difference in time was about three hours, and I had not left my mom's side. The only change that took place was that the Lord showed them that He was stronger than the medications they used to sedate my mom, making it possible for her to speak despite the sedation. The provider also informed me that she was able to go to an ICU step-down, as she was in ICU now. *Wait a moment.* I'm in my head again. *Not only is she medically cleared, but she is also doing better, and they were able to step down her level of care?* They never stop.

Let's do a recap.

How did I get there? I was home in another state when I got a call from a provider letting me know that my mom was about to take her last breath. When I said I was on my way and asked when the rest of the family could be there, I got a call about two hours later saying that my mom was unchanged. The hospital policy stood at only one visitor a day. Call me crazy, but if taking her last breath is the end-of-life, then she was not. They kept her on the same medications for long periods, even though they knew that the medications were damaging her lungs and organs. I forgot to mention that, at some point, they had put my mom on another round of antibiotics and steroids, making it her third round of possible pneumonia. The medications affected her physically as well as mentally. They thought she would die a long time ago. They were helping her preexisting conditions get worse. Ask me why, and my answer is still the same. They used my mom as an undocumented COVID-19 case study. What they didn't know was that my mom was a fighter. It took a toll on her, they broke her down, but she was still fighting. And now, she was able to go to an ICU step-down.

I wanted to clarify so that we were on the same page. I asked: "Would my mom be going to ICU, ICU step-down, or a regular floor?" I was always asking clear questions.

Provider 3 said: "She no longer needs ICU, but she will not be going to a regular floor. Her oxygen levels still needed to be closely monitored."

I informed Provider 3 that I did not want my mom to go back to the PCU unit (ICU step-down) at this hospital.

Later, the case management team came to my mom's room. They were working on the transfer. I wanted to make sure that I was clear and that everyone knew and was on the same page. I informed them that Provider 3 mentioned that my mom could be transferred to an ICU step-down, and I informed them she was not to be transferred back to the " PCU unit (ICU step-down)" at "this hospital." We had many problems on that PCU unit, and my mom was not to come in contact with the nurses or the floor. They informed me that they would let bed placement know. The plan was to transfer her from the ICU to the other facility. We were so excited, humbled, but scared.

Chapter 14

On the day of the transfer, April 23, 2021, my mom was alert and talking. She knew that she was being transferred. I signed the transfer papers. I couldn't ride with her due to the COVID-19 restrictions, but I told her that I would be right behind the ambulance and praying all the way there.

We made it to the other hospital, and my mom was still breathing. We got her all setup, and the ambulance staff was discussing her oxygen with nursing. Then they were asking me how much oxygen she was on at the other hospital. The nurses were still settling her in and started their evaluation of my mom. I was evaluating my mom's room. I didn't see any equipment, and I started getting concerned. I asked where the monitoring system was for her oxygen, blood pressure, and so on. Nursing told me that, on this floor, they have portable units, and she started setting them up. I asked if they were connected to the nursing station so that they also could monitor her. The nurse informed me that they were not, but they come to check frequently. I was a little confused. The accepting provider came into my mom's room. He was asking questions and started logging everything. Then he asked about her oxygen requirements from the other facility and her labs.

I was thinking. *Her oxygen requirements seem to be a hot topic, as everyone is questioning them.*

The provider informed me that he didn't see her oxygen requirements or her labs in her transfer-discharge packet. I logged into her health portal and gave him her reading. He asked if I knew what her feeding amount was for the feeding tube.

I said: "Wait, they didn't send that?"

The provider was searching through the papers, and he said: "Usually everything is right here under the discharge transfer, but there is nothing." Then he told me not to worry.

I was calm but worried. He was going to have respiratory and the dietitian come by. The nurse came back in. She was asking some questions, and there was a little confusion. I informed her that my mom was coming here from ICU.

She said: "ICU?"

I said: "Yes, this is an ICU step-down floor, correct?"

She said: "No."

I was having flashbacks in my head, going over the conversation with Provider 3 at the hospital she transferred from about her transfer, and he assured me that she was going to an ICU step-down, as she was not ready for a regular floor. *What was I thinking?* I knew we couldn't trust them. The transferring hospital will not stop. I called the transfer center at the new accepting hospital. I was concerned, scared, and worried. I voiced my concerns. I was informed that the hospital she transferred from did not send over the information that she needed ICU step-down a higher level of care. She was basically put on a regular floor.

Let's do a recap.

At the old hospital, my mom was in ICU. I was told by Provider 3, her main provider at the old hospital, that she no longer needed the ICU level of care and that she was being lowered to an ICU step-down supposedly when she was transferred to the new hospital. Per Provider 3, because her oxygen levels still needed to be closely monitored, she was not able and ready to be on a regular floor. But the information that the transferring hospital sent over did not support what Provider 3 told me, which is why my mom ended up on a regular floor.

This was all too familiar, as that's what took place at the beginning of her stay. The transfer center informed me that they would pass this information on to the person who would be doing rounds and that they would keep a close eye on her. If she needed a higher level of care, the provider here could change it.

The receiving hospital did a complete evaluation of my mom's body. I shook my head at all of the bumps and bruises. Her bottom was completely raw, from front to back. Her right nostril, where the feeding tube was, was completely blocked with dried, clotted blood.

The system had failed. We need change. *How many more people must go through or have already gone through what my mom endured before the system changes?* I remember talking to my sister about the things that happened and our mom's condition at the hospital she transferred from. My mom had so much phlegm with a horrible cough that we constantly had to suction it out, or she would gag on it. The hospital she transferred from said that it was because of all the fluid she had and the congestive heart failure. When we transferred her to the new hospital, we had the suction ready. I suctioned her about two times before her phlegm and cough went away.

What were they giving her to keep her in such distress? This was like a breath of fresh air. My mom was able to see her providers. Her gospel music was on continuously. She was having frequent visits with the chaplain, and I will never forget one of their conversations. I wanted the chaplain to go over her health care wishes with me again and to talk about a ventilator if one was ever needed. What were her wishes?

Now, remember that Provider 3 at the previous hospital said that she wanted to switch to a DNR. The chaplain at the new hospital asked what her wishes were and her feelings about a ventilator if needed. My mom said: "I had nothing. I had to fight my whole life. I will continue fighting for my family." My mom gave the same answer. She has told me my whole life do whatever it takes; she did not want to be a DNR. Shame on them.

On another occasion, my mom was speaking to the chaplain, and she gave him her book to read. He did, and when he brought it back, they talked about it. He always prayed with her. I remember my sister and I talking to my mom, telling her that she must be around for us, the grands, the great grands, and to write her second book. My mom told my sister and me that she did not have to be around for the next book, as we knew her story. For two days, once overnight, I was informed they had to call rapid response for my mom because of her breathing. The next day when I arrived, I heard them calling rapid response to her room. The chaplain heard it also. He met me there. I asked to speak to the nursing manager. I explained to the nurse manager and the medical team where the disconnect came from the transferring hospital and her level of care to an ICU step-down. I think that, by that time, pulmonary, respiratory, and everyone else was there and agreed that she needed a higher level of care. She was transferred within an hour to a different floor that could accommodate her needs.

Chapter 15

Her transfer was good, and my mom was at peace. The damage that the transferring hospital had caused to my mom's organs and health was already done. My mom was broken to the point of no return. Her condition had gone untreated for far too long, neglecting her labs, not doing anything to try and fix or balance them, and giving her the medications that they knew would cause more damage to her already damaged organs for long periods of time. It took a toll on her, her body, and her organs. They left her with no good working parts to fight with.

No longer constantly sedated, she was able to tell us of her aches and pains. She started telling us that her finger was throbbing. It had a small black dot on it, and she was in so much pain. The new hospital gave her something for pain. In about two days, from the small black dot on the tip of her finger, the whole tip of the finger became black. At that point, we got confirmation from her doctor that it was not good. Her body was not getting enough oxygen, and the tissue in her finger was dying.

The Lord said that my mom had enough, 2 Corinthians chapter 5 verses 8 through 10 NKJV; We are confident, yes, well pleased rather to be absent from the body and to be present with the Lord. She has a new body in heaven, Amen. Let us not forget how we got here.

I returned home, and I reached out again to yet another lawyer. This time, after telling my mom's story, they asked if we had done an autopsy. I said no. Their answer was the same as earlier when I tried to seek help; they were unable to take the case. The law offices never clarified what they meant. Only one of the law offices stated their reasoning, saying that it was not a case they would take on. I remember wondering, was her case was not good enough for them? Was her death not good enough? What difference did it make that we had not had an autopsy performed? Now it feels like it is our fault that we cannot get help because we did not do an autopsy. No one was there to guide us. The system failed. The system must change. No one could help us when she was alive, and now it seems that no one can help us when she is no longer here.

Chapter 16

The family is left trying to put the pieces back together. How can we do that when most of the important pieces are missing? Where are the pieces of peace when there is no peace? We cannot get back my mom, the main piece.

Yes, in time, with my mom's health conditions, she would have passed away from them. But not how and when she did. We would have been sad, heartbroken, hurt, the normal feelings of pain and emptiness. But we could find some comfort in knowing that she was in a better place, with no more pain and no more suffering. Instead, we are left with anger and hurt that will never go away. Why? Because we know how she got to this point, the visions of everything the transferring hospital did to my mom that led to her death. Again, I can speak only about this hospital. Do you understand where I am coming from?

If my mom had passed away under normal circumstances, our loss would still hurt, but, over time, God's comfort and peace would come along. Yes, it just happened. The wound is still fresh.

But, every time I think about my mom's death, no matter how much time has passed, I always go back to how this hospital, the transferring hospital, played a major part in her death. Time cannot, and will not, change that.

No one deserves that. Our family is forever scarred by nightmares, trauma, daze, and confusion. Which way do we go, which way do we turn? We continue to pray. Never in all my years would I have imagined this facility, the transferring hospital, could go against everything they were supposed to stand for. Yes, the transferring hospital is a big corporation, and there are other big corporations that do wrong. Yet, we feel that, because they are so big, it's easy to be intimidated and to believe that nothing can come from it. But we, the people, as a whole, have to stand up and stand together against them no matter our race, religion, culture, social and ethnic backgrounds, gender, or sexual orientation.

Put yourselves in our shoes. This time it was our mom. No one else's mother, father, sister, brother, and so on should ever have to go through what our mom went through. We all bleed the same; it's not rich blood or poor blood; it's just blood. We all should be able to relate; we all started with a mother somewhere somehow.

I look at life through a new set of lenses. We know there is a lot of wrongdoing in the world, and, yes, there is a lot that is good. We don't have to accept the wrongdoing. It's not right, and it's not fair. We need justice for my mom. The transferring hospital should be held accountable, liable for its actions. I am my mom's child, and her blood runs through my veins. What happened to the pledge of allegiance, one nation under God? Ecclesiastes chapter 3 verses 1 through 8. "This is my time to speak, my time to stand." We need justice for my mom. Time won't heal the inhumanity, torture, pain, suffering, neglect, anxiety, and feelings of hopelessness and helplessness that my mom and our family had to endure. We pray for peace, for strength, for forgiveness, and for justice for those who have trespassed against us.

Epilogue

I spoke with a lawyer again, who informed me I would have to find a good civil litigation lawyer. The state in which the transferring hospital is located makes it hard, but not impossible, for malpractice cases. Can you imagine that? I will continue searching until I find a good civil litigation lawyer.

I started writing a letter of complaint and ended up here. This is a true story based on my mother's experiences, misdiagnosed, pain, and suffering at this hospital during the COVID-19 pandemic. Thank you for your time. We are stronger together. Love, peace, and blessings all the time.

In loving memory of our mom's blood, struggle, and tears.
We need justice!
We need change!